INSECTS AS...
INVADERS

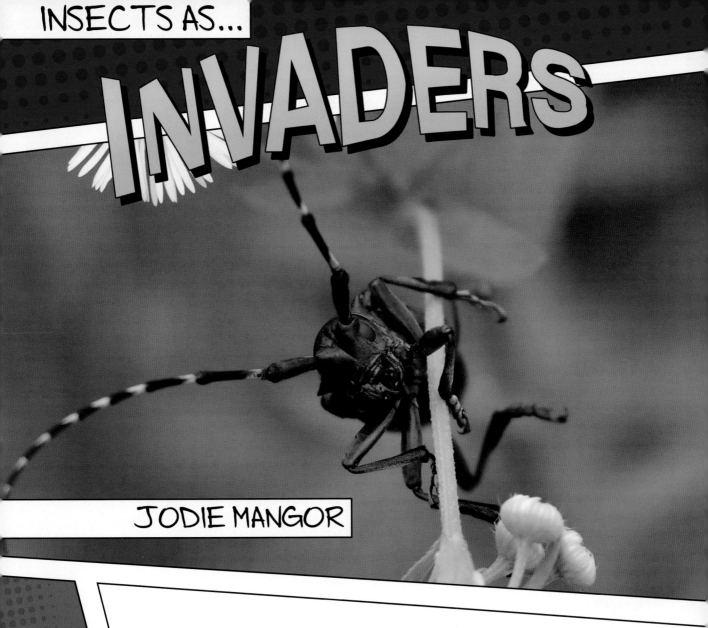

JODIE MANGOR

Rourke
Educational Media

rourkeeducationalmedia.com

Scan for Related Titles
and Teacher Resources

Before Reading:

Building Academic Vocabulary and Background Knowledge

Before reading a book, it is important to tap into what your child or students already know about the topic. This will help them develop their vocabulary, increase their reading comprehension, and make connections across the curriculum.

1. *Look at the cover of the book. What will this book be about?*
2. *What do you already know about the topic?*
3. *Let's study the Table of Contents. What will you learn about in the book's chapters?*
4. *What would you like to learn about this topic? Do you think you might learn about it from this book? Why or why not?*
5. *Use a reading journal to write about your knowledge of this topic. Record what you already know about the topic and what you hope to learn about the topic.*
6. *Read the book.*
7. *In your reading journal, record what you learned about the topic and your response to the book.*
8. *After reading the book complete the activities below.*

Content Area Vocabulary
Use glossary words in a sentence.

application
ballast
deprive
ecosystems
feces
hazards
larvae
native species
predators
resources

After Reading:

Comprehension and Extension Activity

After reading the book, work on the following questions with your child or students in order to check their level of reading comprehension and content mastery.

1. *Name three things you can do if you encounter an invasive insect. (Summarize)*
2. *How did the Asian tiger mosquito get its name? (Infer)*
3. *How were fire ants originally transported from South America to the U.S.? (Asking questions)*
4. *In what ways can invasive insects cause problems for people? (Text to self connection)*
5. *What do invasive insects do to damage forests and businesses? (Asking questions)*

Extension Activity

Invasive insects can cause a lot of problems to natural habitats. Using construction paper and colored pencils, draw some of the invasive insects you read about in the book and label your pictures with the damage these insects cause. Use other sources, such as the Internet, to find out even more about these creepy crawlers that invade and damage our environment.

Table of Contents

Like It or Not, Here They Come!

For each person on Earth, there are 200 million bugs. Most of these insects live in balanced **ecosystems**. But if they are moved from their natural home to a new habitat, they may become invasive.

Invasive insects spread quickly, taking over habitats and ruining them for **native species**. Eventually, these pests may crowd out or kill local organisms.

Nutria

What is an invasive species? It is a living thing that does not naturally occur in an ecosystem. When introduced, it causes harm to that ecosystem.

Not all invasive species are insects. Invasive plants, fish, mammals, and more all affect our natural ecosystems. Kudzu (a climbing vine), Asian carp, and furry nutria are just a few examples.

Human activity helps to spread invasive insects from one location to another. Sometimes bugs are brought to a new place on purpose, in hopes that they will help solve a problem, such as control an existing invader. Other times, they are moved by accident.

Invasive insects or their **larvae**, or eggs, can hide in plant material and cargo. They are then transported around the world by ships, planes, and land vehicles. They can even catch a ride on a traveler's clothes or luggage!

A single female insect can lay hundreds or even thousands of eggs during its lifetime.

When invasive insects move into a new area, there are no natural **predators** to keep them in check. Native species have no defenses against them. This allows their population to grow quickly.

As their numbers climb, these bugs use up important **resources**. They change an area's food web by destroying or replacing native food sources and eating up native species.

Insect invaders can also be health **hazards**, potentially spreading disease to native species and humans.

Invasive species pose problems around the world. They threaten our crops, forests, homes, and health. Every year, the United States spends billions of dollars trying to prevent, detect, and control insect invaders. Often, there are no easy solutions.

Forest Pests

Invasive insects affect forests all over the world. They have spread far and wide, hidden in wooden pallets, crates, and packaging.

These pests kill trees so we can no longer enjoy their natural beauty or shade. They **deprive** animals of their habitats, and businesses of the wood they need to make products.

A NEW ARRIVAL: CASE OF THE SPOTTED LANTERNFLY

The spotted lanternfly is new to the United States. This Asian native was first detected in Pennsylvania in 2014. It feeds on many types of trees. If it spreads, it could affect both fruit orchards and logging operations.

CREEPY CATERPILLARS: CASE OF THE EUROPEAN GYPSY MOTH

In a heavily infected area, you can hear European gypsy moth larvae chewing. They eat the leaves of more than 300 different tree species.

Gypsy moth caterpillars can strip a tree bare. So far, more than 75 million acres (303,514.23 square kilometers) in the United States have been affected by gypsy moths.

Amazingly, this destructive pest was brought to the United States on purpose! In the 1800s, a French scientist brought a small number of gypsy moths to Massachusetts, with the hopes of breeding them to make cheap silk. A few escaped, starting a major invasion. Gypsy moth outbreaks are difficult to control, even with pesticide **application**.

Gypsy moth caterpillars can spread by ballooning. New larvae spin a thread at the end of a tree branch and dangle from it. They are caught by the wind, which carries them away to a new location.

ASIAN INVADERS!
CASE OF THE EMERALD ASH BORER

The emerald ash borer, a sleek, glittery green beetle, comes from northern China and Korea. It was first discovered in the United States and Canada in 2002. It most likely came over in wood used for shipping.

In Asia, trees are resistant to the emerald ash borer and predators help keep it in check. But in North America, there are no natural controls.

Asian parasitic wasps that attack emerald ash borer larvae may help to control this pest.

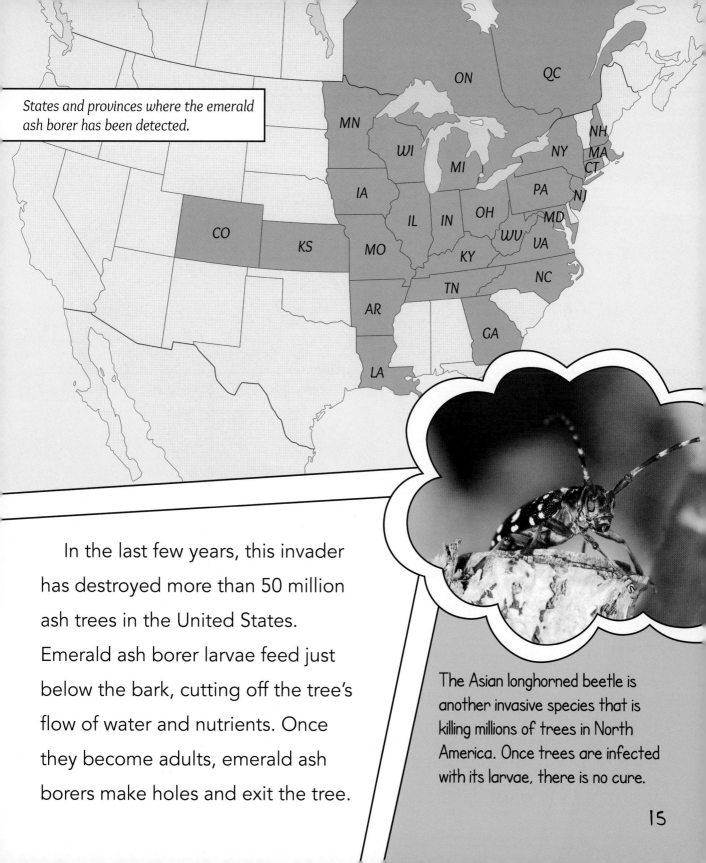

States and provinces where the emerald ash borer has been detected.

In the last few years, this invader has destroyed more than 50 million ash trees in the United States. Emerald ash borer larvae feed just below the bark, cutting off the tree's flow of water and nutrients. Once they become adults, emerald ash borers make holes and exit the tree.

The Asian longhorned beetle is another invasive species that is killing millions of trees in North America. Once trees are infected with its larvae, there is no cure.

Crop Pests

Invasive insects can have dramatic effects on crops and farmland. Farmers spend millions of dollars annually trying to protect what they grow. Still, each year, insect pests cost the United States $13 billion in crop loss and $2.1 billion in forest damage.

FROM GOOD TO BAD: CASE OF THE HARLEQUIN LADYBUG

The harlequin ladybug was brought to Europe and North America from Asia, with hopes that it would protect plants by eating the aphids that feed on them.

It did this job well. But soon it began eating the eggs and larvae of native ladybug species, causing their numbers to drop. It is now considered a serious invader.

The harlequin ladybug has a secret weapon: a deadly fungus that lives in its blood. If other types of ladybugs try to eat it, the fungus kills them.

CASE OF THE LIGHT BROWN APPLE MOTH

The light brown apple moth comes from Australia. This plain-looking pest first appeared in the United States in 2007, in California. It consumes about 250 crops, including apple, grape, cherry, and many vegetables.

Light brown apple moth caterpillars look similar to many other species. They roll leaves into hiding places, making them hard to find and control.

CASE OF THE ASIAN CITRUS PYSLLID

The Asian citrus pysllid feasts on the leaves and stems of citrus trees. As it feeds, this pinhead-sized invader spreads bacteria that cause a disease called citrus greening.

There is no known cure for citrus greening. Most infected trees die within a few years. The United States Department of Agriculture has spent hundreds of millions of dollars in search of a cure.

NOT SO SWEET: CASE OF THE SWEET POTATO WHITEFLY

The sweet potato whitefly is a tiny sap-sucking insect thought to have originated from India or the Middle East.

After more than 100 years in the United States, it has only recently become a serious pest. It feeds on more than 500 species of plants, damaging crops such as tomatoes, peppers, watermelon, and cotton. It can also carry and spread over a hundred different plant viruses.

Whiteflies are mostly found on the undersides of leaves. Adults are just 0.04 inches (1 millimeter) long.

The sweet potato whitefly makes a sugary waste called honeydew. It gets on cotton fibers and makes them hard to process. It also allows a mold to grow. It's hard to clean off produce, reducing its quality.

People Pests

Some invasive insects pester people. They bite and sting, spread disease, and generally bother us.

OUR HOME IS THEIR HOME: CASE OF THE GERMAN COCKROACH

Despite their name, German cockroaches are originally from Asia. These creepy crawlers are now found throughout the world. In the United States, they are the most common type of cockroach.

German cockroaches are always found near humans. They eat our food, ruining it with their **feces** and vomit. It's even been said that they will eat food off people's faces while they sleep!

German cockroaches carry up to 50 different human diseases.

23

FEISTY FIGHTERS:
CASE OF THE IMPORTED FIRE ANT

Imported fire ants are known for their painful, stinging bites. Swarms can kill small animals. Originally from South America, these aggressive ants were carried to Alabama in the early 1900s, in **ballast** soil on cargo ships.

A fire ant colony can contain 500,000 ants. A queen ant can lay up to 5,000 eggs per day. Ants are found on every continent except Antarctica.

These ants build large nests in agricultural fields, where they are a nuisance and feed on crops. They also like to chew on electrical wires.

Scientists have imported tiny phorid flies from South America. They lay eggs in the fire ant's body. The fly maggots make the ant's head fall off and then eat its brain.

BUSY BITERS: CASE OF THE ASIAN TIGER MOSQUITO

The Asian tiger mosquito is smaller than other mosquitos. It is also more aggressive, and its bite is worse. It prefers to feed during the day rather than at night.

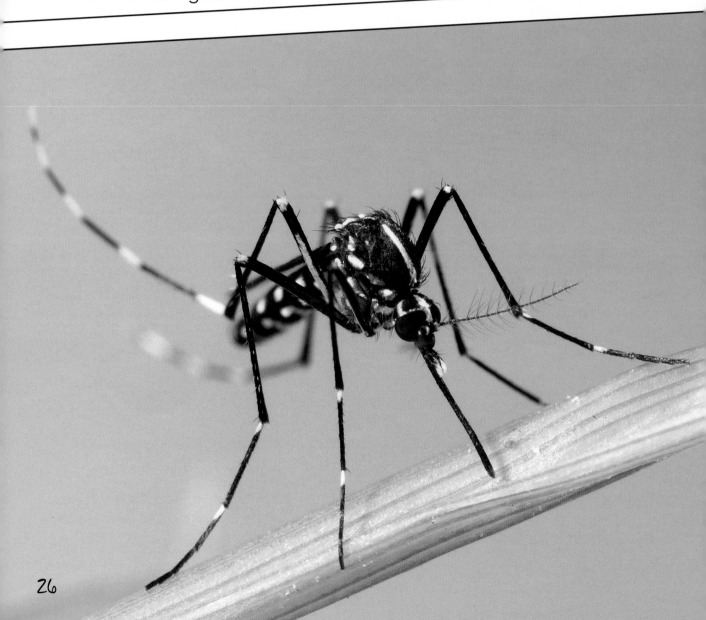

Brought to Texas in 1985 in shipments of used tires, the Asian tiger mosquito is short-lived and can't move far. Still, it has spread to 26 states by laying its eggs in small amounts of standing water in tires, pots, and other containers, which are then moved around.

In Asia, the tiger mosquito carries serious diseases that can infect humans and animals, such as horses and dogs. So far, it has not spread disease in the United States.

27

THE BOTTOM LINE

Invasive insects change ecosystems. They threaten and sometimes kill off native species, pose health risks, and harm agriculture and business, costing nations billions of dollars each year. Around the world, steps are being taken to keep them from spreading.

WHAT CAN YOU DO TO HELP?

- Find out what pests threaten your area.
- Learn how to identify them.
- Check the rules and laws before moving wood or other plant material from one area to another.
- If you see an invasive insect, have someone help you report it to the nearest United States Department of Agriculture office.
- Help spread the word about invasive species.

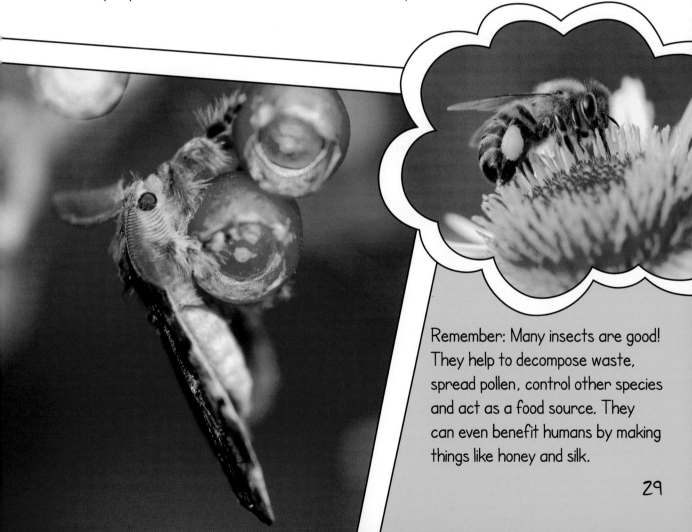

Remember: Many insects are good! They help to decompose waste, spread pollen, control other species and act as a food source. They can even benefit humans by making things like honey and silk.

Glossary

application (ap-li-KAY-shuhn): the act of applying something

ballast (BAL-uhst): heavy material that is put on a ship to make it more stable

deprive (de-PRIVE): to take something away

ecosystems (EE-koh-sis-tuhms): communities of living things interacting with their environment

feces (FEE-sees): solid waste released from a living creature

hazards (HAZ-urds): sources of danger

larvae (LAHR-vee): young insects at a stage where they often look like worms

native species (NAY-tiv SPEE-sheez): animals or plants that live or grow naturally in a particular place

predators (PRED-uh-tuhrz): animals that live by killing and eating other animals for food

resources (REE-sors-ehs): things that are of value or use

Index

Show What You Know

1. Name at least three invasive insects that can be found in the United States.
2. What are two factors that allow an invasive insect to spread quickly in a new habitat?
3. How do invasive insects affect the ecosystems they invade?
4. Name three ways that invasive insects cost nations money.
5. What are some of the ways that invasive insects are spread from one location to another?

Websites to Visit

http://education.nationalgeographic.org/encyclopedia/invasive-species

www.pestworldforkids.org/home

www.invasivespeciesinfo.gov/animals/main.shtml

About The Author

Jodie Mangor writes magazine articles and books for children. She is also the author of audio tour scripts for high-profile museums and tourist destinations around the world. Many of these tours are for kids. She lives in Ithaca, New York, with her family.

www.rourkeeducationalmedia.com

PHOTO CREDITS: Cover: © thatreec, npine; Page 1: © Mark Amy; Page 3: © Mark Bridger; Page 4: © Vladimir Salman; Page 5: © feather collecter, Volodymyr Burdiak; Page 6: © Henrik Larsson; Page 7: © tcly; Page 8: © Patricia Chumilias; Page 9: © Jung_Rattanisiri; Page 10: © Rainer Fuhrmann; Page 11: © Lawrence Barringer - Department of Agriculture; Page 12: © Elliotte Rusty Harold; Page 13: © alexsuirid, Beth Schroeder; Page 14: © Brian Sullivan - USDA Bugwood.org, Debbie Milller - USDA Forest Service; Page 15: © feather collector; Page 16: © Mopparat Promtha; Page 17: © kurt_G, Andre Mueller; Page 18: © Ian Grainger, crazystocker; Page 19: © Jeffrey W. Lotz; Page 20: © D. Kucharsk K. Kucharsk; Page 21: © Bildagentur Zoonar GmbH, David B. Langston - UGA Bugwood.org; Page 22: © Klanarong Chitmung; Page 23: © Erick Karits; Page 24: © smereka; Page 25: © NatalieJean, Siriporn Schwendener; Page 26: © InsectWorld; Page 27: © InsectWorld, dragi52; Page 28: © Michaeljung; Page 29: © thatreec, Ratikova

Edited by: Keli Sipperley
Cover and Interior design by: Tara Raymo www.creativelytara.com

Library of Congress PCN Data

Insects as Invaders / Jodie Mangor
(Insects As ...)
ISBN (hard cover)(alk. paper) 978-1-68191-690-3
ISBN (soft cover) 978-1-68191-791-7
ISBN (e-Book) 978-1-68191-889-1
Library of Congress Control Number: 2016932566

Printed in the United States of America, North Mankato, Minnesota

Also Available as: